2004 PRESIDENTIAL ADDRESS

CONFESSIONS OF A PLATFORMTICKETAHOLIC

given by

LES DENCH

To a meeting of the Society at
London Road Station, Brighton,
on 19th February 2005
and subsequently repeated at
European Inn,
Midland Road,
Derby
on 16th April 2005

The Transport Ticket Society
2011

*The production of this publication has also been made possible thanks
to the bequest to the Society by the late Courtney Haydon
who was a member for about 34 years*

*Further copies of this and other Publications may be obtained from the
Society's Publication Sales Officer:*

Steve Skeavington
6 Breckbank,
Forest Town,
MANSFIELD.
NG19 0PZ

*Comments etc. regarding this publication are welcome;
please write to the Hon. Secretary,*

Alan Peachey
4 The Sycamores,
BISHOPS STORTFORD.
CM23 5JR

Published by

The Transport Ticket Society
4 The Sycamores,
Bishops Stortford.
CM23 5JR.

© Les Dench 2011

ISBN 978-0-903209-67-0

Printed by

Pureprint Group
Bellbrook Park
UCKFIELD
TN22 1PL

CONFESSIONS OF A PLATFORMTICKETAHOLIC

Introduction

Thank you for your confidence in voting for me as President at last year's AGM. After you've accepted the honour, of course, you get to find out what you've let yourself in for! There are "Guidelines" for the Presidential Address such as the timing should be around one to one and a half hours, and illustrated. As to subject matter, I recall the Chairman's questions and my responses went something like this:

> "Will it be rail-orientated?" "Er - yes."
> "Will it embrace Europe?" "Er - yes."

Apart from that, the incumbent is reasonably free to choose the subject, except that it should be either:-
   (a) a research theme with potential follow-up, for example as Steve (Skeavington) gave us last year, or
   (b) something else.

Mine's definitely something else. So after three Lord Mayor's Shows you've got me.

Whilst I'm quite used to giving slide shows in this room a "command performance" is a bit more daunting. Oh, and I don't do monologues. Have you ever been to those lectures where, five minutes after it starts, you think of something you'd like to ask, then spend the next fifty-five trying to remember your question and not listening to the talk? I don't function that way, in fact, I prefer audience participation. I might even get some facts wrong so please correct me, and that way both of us may learn something as we go along, but if it gets out of hand Brian (Boddy) will shout "Order!" I should perhaps also explain that most of the narrative reflects my own interpretation of this vast subject, and for authoritative descriptions and listings I would refer you to the various TTS Handbooks by Michael Stewart relating to both British and Overseas platform tickets, and to Godfrey Croughton's work on Irish Platform Tickets [available from the Society's Publications Officer.]

So I'll assume my customary position behind the projector.

CHAPTER 1 - SCHOOL DAYS AND FAMILY HOLIDAYS

A lot of good and bad habits start at school, in my case Varndean (when it was separate Boys and Girls in the late 'forties / early 'fifties). I recall being one of several "trainspotters" from the cliff-top fence in Terminus Road overlooking Brighton steam shed. Our interests gradually moved into luggage labels and platform tickets. Brighton Enquiry Office (precursor to today's Travel Centres) had a rack of labels which included many still headed London, Brighton & South Coast Railway, and up to now I have never documented anything in respect of Platform Tickets, mainly because of there being other far more knowledgeable TTS members than I who have done so. All that I have penned was a short article in two railway paperwork journals a couple of years ago on Collecting LB&SCR Luggage Labels, recounting those exploits which involved several form-mates, the Headmaster, and the British Transport Police. However, there were no such problems with platform tickets as we bought them rather than stole them. For many years the collection comprised only those which I had bought personally, and in 1950, of course, there was no existing documentation of types or issuing stations.

An exhibition of tickets by Gordon Fairchild in Hove Library I think in August 1952 caught my eye, so I duly made contact, and joined the Ticket and Fare Collection Society (as it was then) in September or October 1952, and have been able to verify the date from Roger Atkinson's tribute to Stan Hughes in January [2004] *Journal* which states that there were 104 members by the end of 1952. (TTS membership records are apparently unable to confirm joining dates in the 1950s.)

Not surprisingly we started around our local area.

1–1

1-1 Preston Park No. 2, in those days was a proper station with up and down ticket offices, and here we discovered an older specimen, which we later got to learn was a type 2. [1951]

1-2 Hassocks D.O. also 1951. This was the only type to be designated Hassocks D.O. [Down Office], all other Southern Railway and British Railways issues being Hassocks No. 2.

1-2

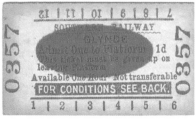

1-3

1-4

1-3 and 1-4 Glynde and Berwick are type 1 variants of the familiar "red blob" of early SR, and, of course, the LBSCR before them. It is interesting to note that two adjacent stations showed printing varieties! I must also just explain here that some of the tickets illustrated are better copies obtained in later years, as many originals were not in best condition having been "faced up" in the ticket racks when I could only afford to buy one at a time.

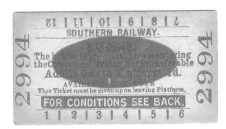

1– 5

1-5 On 12th September 1950, at the tender age of 14, I embarked on a one-day 80 mile bike ride Brighton - Lewes - Horsted Keynes - East Grinstead - Three Bridges - Horsham - Steyning - Brighton and uncovered some more gems. Barcombe is yet another variant on the type 1 theme.

1-6

1-7

1-6 The next station up the line was the long-forgotten Newick and Chailey, whilst **1-7** Horsted Keynes is still with us in the guise of the Bluebell Railway. The final closure by B.R. of the Lewes / East Grinstead line came in March 1958, and the embryonic preserved Bluebell Railway enjoyed their first passengers in August 1960.

1-8

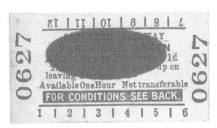

1-9

1-8 Turning left at East Grinstead, next illustrated is Rowfant, which is perhaps noteworthy for it being the only SR issue the station ever had. 0017 is clearly dated 12 SP 50, so I wonder when the sale of these actually commenced?

1-9 One example from the Horsham / Shoreham line is Partridge Green. I'm now finding these "red blobs" all over Sussex, and hardly two are exactly the same.

1-10

1-10 The opportunity arose for participation in a School trip in April/May 1952, by cycle and ferry to Belgium and Holland staying in Youth Hostels - no jetting off to ski resorts in those days! We crossed from Dover to Ostend and the first priority was to see if they had platform tickets. Yes, but only the rather anonymous "7969" which I duly noted was Ostend Quai station.

1-11

1-12

1-11, 1-12 During the week as circumstances permitted I occasionally broke away from the main party and looked around a few stations. Just a couple of examples here, Den Haag Staatsspoor and Fyenoord, the latter having some significance to the football fraternity, I gather. All examples obtained that week were of the then current 10¢ variety. [See 11-20 to 11-23 for older types obtained much more recently.]

1-13

1-13 Back nearer home some family holidays enabled visits to endangered branch lines, as much to ride over them as to obtain platform tickets. The priority was Hythe (Kent) which had a very sparse service, had been cut back from Sandgate in 1931, and closed itself in December 1951. My solo day out was on 7 August 1950.

1-14

1-15

1-14, 1-15 In the summer of 1953 we holidayed in the Isle of Wight, and news of forthcoming closures ensured I went again on 19 September 1953 for the last day of the Freshwater and Bembridge lines. [For further tickets from the Isle of Wight see illustrations 4-9, 4-10 and 5-2].

CHAPTER 2 - DISCOVERING IRELAND 1957/58

As the 'fifties decade proceeds it is apparent that the pastime of collecting platform tickets is becoming addictive but is frequently linked to travelling over branch and secondary railway lines before they are closed. In 1957 and 1958 we made voyages of discovery to Ireland, where everything, including the pace of life, seemed to be many years behind the English mainland that we were used to. Prompted mainly by the wholesale closure of the Great Northern of Ireland's cross-border lines, there were also some organised rail tours both within Ireland and by groups from Britain.

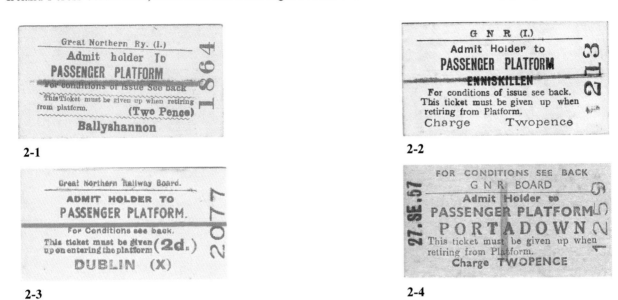

2-1

2-2

2-3

2-4

2-1, 2-2, 2-3 and **2-4**   The first shock was to find a price tag of 2d, double that of mainland Britain! Even three contemporary GNR show differences such as "when *retiring* from the platform", whilst the Dublin issue states "when *entering* platform". GNR issues bore a thin red line overprint, and the Great Northern Railway (Ireland) became the Great Northern Railway Board on 1st September 1953. The four illustrated were obtained in September 1957, showing that "pre-nat" issues could still be found just as they were back nearer home.

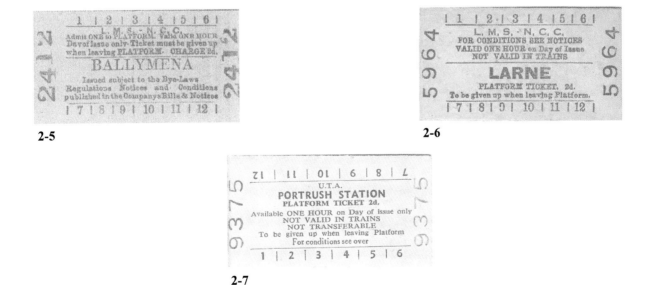

2-5

2-6

2-7

2-5, 2-6 and **2-7** With historical precedents some lines in Northern Ireland had come under the "umbrella" of the Midland Railway (of England) as the "Northern Counties Committee" and, of course, subsequently the London, Midland & Scottish Railway, so it is not surprising that LMS-NCC examples are much like the latter-day LMSR, whilst the UTA [Ulster Transport Authority, which the LMS-NCC became in 1948] is close to a BR type 2.

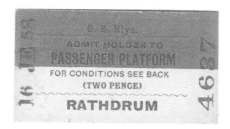

2-8

2-9

2-10

2-8, **2-9** and **2-10** Further down south in the Irish Free State, apart from the Great Northern, most railways were grouped into the Great Southern Railways on 1st January 1925 , and nationalised as the Córas Iompair Éireann on 1st January 1945. **2-8** shows a latter-day GSR from Rathdrum, **2-9** an early CIE from Wicklow, and **2-10** Bray a later type from the CIE, all issued in 1957 and 1958.

CHAPTER 3 - BRANCH LINE CLOSURES

I have already referred to travel habits in the previous chapter, and the phenomenon continued unabated into the 'sixties, and even in much more recent times as you will see at 3-9 and 3-10.

3-1

3-1 Gravesend West Street is from a last day / last train visit I made on 1 August 1953.

3-2

3-2 The last day of service on the Alexandra Palace branch occurred on 3 July 1954, when I was lucky enough to purchase platform ticket number 1999 which is too grubby to illustrate here. John Britton had number 1998 (which recently appeared at an auction) and he remarked at the time, and indeed in subsequent years, that the London & North Eastern Railway's 1924 supply of 2000 tickets neatly lasted for 30 years until the final closure day.

3-3

3-4

3-3 Hawkhurst closed on 12 June 1961 but the ticket is one I bought in May.

3-4 West Hoathly's last train day was actually 28 May 1955 then there was a 2½ week ASLEF [train drivers' union] strike, although the line re-opened, but closed again on 16 March 1958.

3-5

3-6

3-5, 3-6 The Bundoran branch, in the west of Ireland, lost its services at the end of September 1957 [see also 2-1 for the next station up the line], and Harcourt Street (Dublin) on the first day of 1959.

3-7

3-8

3-7, 3-8 Another Irish pair - Warrenpoint's last day was 2 January 1965, with 5408 being issued on that day, whilst Youghal closed on 4 February 1963.

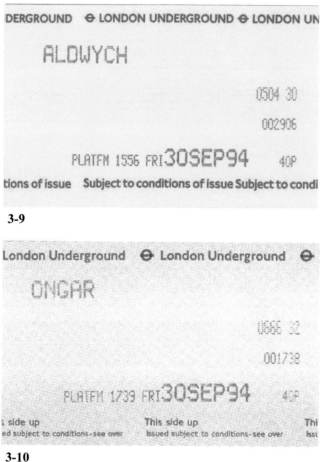

3-9

3-10

3-9, 3-10 This is not all about 'fifties and 'sixties closures by any means - 30 September 1994 was a busy day as well, this time on the London Transport Underground, and even many of our younger members will have been there too! **3-9** Aldwych, and **3-10** Ongar.

CHAPTER 4 - BEING IN THE RIGHT PLACE AT THE RIGHT TIME

The 'fifties were a time of great change, and just occasionally I had called at a station on the very day that old stocks ran out.

4-1   **4-2**

4-1 and **4-2**   Bramber were obtained on 23 February 1952.

4-3   **4-4**

4-3 and **4-4**   Waldron & Horam date from September and October 1951, and note how the station name became abbreviated, then later still it was further shortened to just plain Horam. The difference of 1000 tickets could not apparently be accounted for, unless perhaps a supply of SR type 3 had been on hand and were never used?

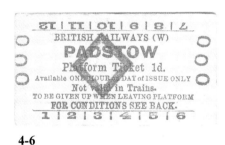

4-5   **4-6**

4-5 and **4-6**   Somewhat further away from home I was lucky at Padstow 18 January 1952, and this was from the (geographical) end of the Southern Railway, literally, as it became part of BR's Western Region.

4-7   **4-8**

4-7 and **4-8**   Even in 1988 I repeated my luck at Liverpool Street underground station in London. (For my own involvement at BR's Liverpool Street see chapter 9.2, illustrations 9-6 to 9-12.)

4-9

4-10

4-9 and **4-10** And on one occasion, when there's no platform ticket on issue, it seemed to be the obvious thing to do to buy a ticket to the next station, so at Watchingwell on 19 September 1953, the last day of passenger service, at 3.30 p.m., a unique changeover on a single ticket. An SR one sold at auction a couple of years ago for ... quite a lot, but there cannot have been many BR ones issued! [see also 5-2]

CHAPTER 5 - THE TRUTH ABOUT THOSE "FORGERIES" . . . WELL, ALMOST

Once upon a time there were three school chums, John, Peter and yours truly, of cliff-top trainspotting and luggage label pilfering fame as already mentioned in my introduction. After some rather varied exam results, we all joined BR at different times, John and Peter starting in booking offices at Southwick and Burgess Hill. A little while later I moved to Waterloo HQ, and discovered George, another collector of tickets, who had connections and knew people in the right places. So in April 1956 a private visit was arranged to the Southern Region ticket printing works at Deepdene, where I believe we gathered up printers' waste, gained a few "audit" tickets from closed stations, and persuaded one or two printers to do things they probably shouldn't have done.

5-1

5-2

5-3

5-4

5-1, 5-2, 5-3, 5-4   George and I printed Holland Road Halt and Watchingwell (note similarity of type and serial numbers,) whilst John and Peter I know for sure did Ventnor West, but for a long time I could not be convinced about Bulford as I only had two or three, whilst having more spares of the others. As we have long since lost touch, and George being older at the time may well no longer be with us, absolute confirmation is not possible, but examination by Michael Stewart of known serial numbers must put it in this category. Note specially on the day that three types were still being printed concurrently.

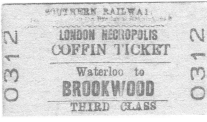

5-5

5-6

5-6

5-5, 5-6   There were old bits of type including some dating from LBSCR days, and unusual categories, just lying there, waiting to be used again (!), so the temptation to print a Coffin ticket was overwhelming, as well as the chance to include a typical LBSCR destination style on a modern ticket.

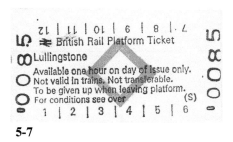

5-7

5-7 Lullingstone is one of many "green diamonds" which never got to stations (especially when never fully built, let alone opened), and one of our prominent members (who resides in Kent) knows something about that one, along with several other stations!

5-8   **5-9**

5-8 and **5-9** Many years later, an official TTS visit to Crewe on 23 September 1987 resulted in South Gyle, possibly my instigation again unless, of course, I was egged on by others which sounds like a good excuse. Certainly a case of *déjà-vu*! Note also that as we were then becoming used to red-print platform tickets with green diamonds we just had to have one of each.

CHAPTER 6 - WITH A LITTLE HELP FROM MY FRIENDS (AND RELATIONS)

In the earliest collecting days platform tickets were very much of my own purchase at the stations concerned, but sooner or later I realised that I could not get all of them that way, so in order to help the collection grow I enlisted the help of friends and even relations, especially those travelling to far flung parts of the world such as India, which not surprisingly is very British influenced.

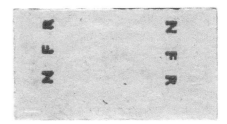

6-1

6-1 The front and back of Darjeeling, on the much reported and photographed North East Frontier Railway. It is generally the custom in India for the railway company's initials to appear on ticket backs.

6-2

6-2 Islampur, on the Futwah Islampur Light Railway. On the back is "M L R" which helpfully tells us that the operator was Martins Light Railways.

6-3

6-3 Inflation catches up with Mobha Road on the Western Railway by January 1993 - the price has been altered once by rubber stamp and five times in ink!

6-4

6-4 My brother went to Egypt in 1959 for what is now called students' "gap year" so was given instructions beforehand. He went to many other places, but did at least manage to get platform tickets from three or four stations in that country for me.

6-5

6-5 Sousse (Tunisia) is so French, especially the "Penalty" clause warning of the dire "verbal process" if you dared to set foot in a train!

6-6

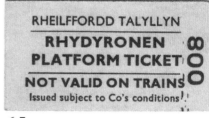

6-7

6-6, 6-7 Having known one of the Traffic Assistants on the Talyllyn Railway for very many years he was conveniently on hand for the railway's extension to Nant Gwernol in 1976, and the first issue at Rhydyronen in 1983, the latter printed by Michael Farr. Coincidentally it was this same colleague who acquired the FIL for me illustrated at 6-2.

CHAPTER 7 - EXPLORING EUROPE - HOLIDAYS AND EXCURSIONS

From around the late 'sixties we enjoyed various family holidays, this time my wife and I with our boys, rather than the previous generation as recounted in Chapter One, which enabled platform tickets to be acquired personally from other parts of Europe.

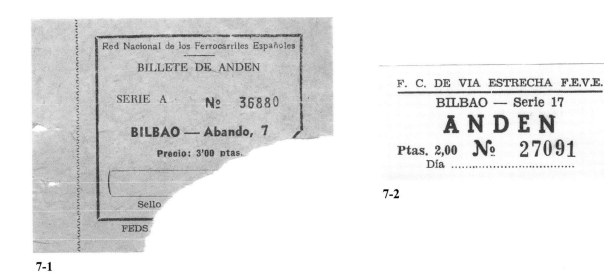

7-1

7-2

7-1 and **7-2** are both from terminal stations in Bilbao in northern Spain. Bilbao Abando is the RENFE (Spanish National Railways) main line station, whilst the FEVE (Spanish Narrow Gauge Railways) was issued at its Achuri terminus, these representing two of Bilbao's six stations.

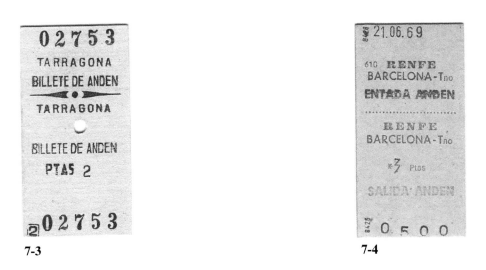

7-3

7-4

7-3 and **7-4** are from Mediterranean coastal towns in Spain, and illustrate pre-printed and Multiprinter types. Note the prices varied even then at 2 or 3 pesetas, and the tickets are designed to be torn in half - but only if actually going onto the platform, of course. [1967 and 1969]

```
11-05-84      9-59   247191797
HOVE
TOEGANG TOT DE PERRONS
GELDIG 1 UUR
                        ××××10F
```

7-5

```
16-03-87      8-53   346009510
UCCLE-CALEVOET
ACCES AUX QUAIS
VALABLE 1 HEURE
                        ××××10F
```

7-6

```
16-03-87      8-54   346009511
UKKEL-KALEVOET
TOEGANG TOT DE PERRONS
GELDIG 1 UUR
                        ××××10F
```

7-7

7-5, 7-6 and **7-7** Belgium was mostly ProData machine issues by the mid-eighties. I couldn't resist the Hove which I have always thought was next door to Brighton (!) and note too the bi-lingual machine capability with consecutively numbered Uccle / Ukkel issues of one in each language. Issue of platform tickets ceased in Belgium soon after April 1992.

7-8

7-9

7-8 and **7-9** Moving to France, the SATAS coin-operated machine was provided at many stations, made purchase easy and avoided any possible language problems. It came in two varieties: Abbeville with 1-niche, and Nice 2 -niche.

7-10 **7-11**

7-10 and **7-11** The Synthegra was a ticket office machine, and also came in two varieties: one - Bordeaux, [21 February 1984] whilst the other had "tariff boxes". Note specially the one from Bâle, priced in Swiss Francs, available from a separate ticket window located at the entrance to the French part of the station, obtained 15 March 1980, only the final figure of the year being shown.

7-12 and **7-13** The rather more prolific French issues were the red edge Edmondsons, which in various guises (and prices) had been around since before "New Franc" days of 1960 and indeed before I ever set foot in France. La Tour de Carol [1985] is a later example from the "compostage" era (self-cancellation at ticket barriers), and even one from Monaco-Monte Carlo obtained in 1983, which of course has an SNCF station. [See Chapter 11 for older tickets acquired in later years.]

7-12 **7-13**

7-14 **7-15**

7-14 and **7-15** Another type of ticket office machine was the CGA [Compagnie General d'Automatique] used mostly in the Paris suburban area, as exemplified by Roissy Aeroport [February 1981]. The one from Versailles [May 1980] I think was a coin in slot machine, possibly an advanced SATAS. The issue of platform tickets in France ceased completely around 1989/90.

7-16

7-17

7-16 and **7-17** We only made two visits to Luxembourg (in 1986) by which time I think only Luxembourg City remained as an issuing station, with Multiprinters in the booking office, and a Rapidprinter coin-in-the-slot machine on the wall of the ticket hall.

7-18

7-19

7-20

7-18, 7-19, 7-20 Italy in the nineteen-eighties only had issues remaining from Milano, Torino, Roma and Palermo. The Rome example is a "flimsy" and a bit disappointing. Subsequently the "pad" variety was available from kiosks situated right by the ticket barriers. These were then modified for "compostage" as introduced by their French neighbours, the same arrangement as for travel tickets. Over the few years of my visits from 1982 the prices went up from Lire 300 - 400 - 500 - 600 - 1000, so at the then equivalent of 50p I made my last purchase of them in 1987. As far as I know they did not survive into the next decade either.

7-21

7-21 is a special Free Platform Ticket for an ETR train exhibition, a new generation of fast electric train which as we all know arrived in France and Italy long before they did in this country!

CHAPTER 8 - MAKING ENDS MEET

The years of raising a young family and being a bit "hard-up" is I'm sure a familiar scene for some of you, and in my case had contrasting effects on my interests. On the down side, it seems that I thinned down my platform tickets in favour of a "stations" collection comprising (preferably) single tickets, a situation from which I did not really recover until retirement (see chapter 11), and shame to admit, I let my membership lapse. But a new phase came along, the effects of which I could not have foreseen. Whilst I was desperate for money, the Southern Region of BR was desperate to keep ticket offices open during evenings and weekends, and the opportunity arose for 'admin' office staff, if they so wished, to perform some of these "unsocial hours" on an overtime basis. So after a half-day training session, over the next few years I found myself "working" at many stations between Polegate and Pulborough, as well as Waterloo, Weybridge, and several suburban stations in between. Fortunes in both senses took a turn for the better as this period also saw the arrival of the 'green diamond' overprints which were first reported in October 1977 *Journal*, and I rejoined the Society in early 1978, which had, by then, become the TTS.

Another classic case of *déjà vu* also presented itself, with occasional opportunities for some 999/000 changes of type which I had previously experienced many years before (see Chapter 4) the difference being that this time I had visual early warning of them happening.

8-1

8-2

8-1 and **8-2** are from Hinchley Wood in January 1979.

8-3

8-4

8-3 and **8-4** are from Queens Road, Battersea, with re-naming to Queenstown Road, which I obtained on 1st May 1981, albeit this time with help from a colleague, the Chief Booking Clerk at Waterloo, whose area of responsibility included Queens Road.

CHAPTER 9 - LIFE ON THE INSIDE

9.1   FILLING A FEW GAPS ON THE GREAT EASTERN

A promotional move from the Southern Region to the Eastern Region, firstly in Revenue Section which among other things dealt with ticket machine parts, such as changing Flexiprinter bits on fares increase days, then later as Acting Area Marketing Manager, had a two-way effect. On the one hand I could obviously not perform ticket office duties on the region I had just left, and fares revision Sundays were considered to be part of the managerial working week, but conversely I was now officially allowed to go inside any ticket office in the Liverpool St Division area. So very gradually, with I hope not appearing to be too "cranky", I took steps to ensure the preservation and interest of our hobby.

9-1

9-2

9-1   My first success was at Prittlewell. Upon enquiring innocently why they hadn't got platform tickets, it was explained to me that "a public footpath runs through the station". I expressed the view that this should not make any difference, so stock was ordered and issue started in January 1983.

9-2   Hatfield Peverel had apparently not had any platform tickets since LNER days, so "instructions" were given and their issue commenced in October 1985.

9-3

9-3   The final issue at Lea Bridge was the unpriced BR red diamond, but although unstaffed since 1976 the station was still open for passengers. The first batch ordered went astray en route and replacements arrived on 10 April 1986, after closure, so the only option was to sell them at Stratford, which may have upset a few purists, but they all went, so somebody must have bought them.

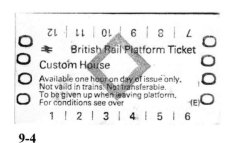

9-4

9-5

9-4, 9-5   The North Woolwich branch stations seemed deserving of a new supply in September 1985, and this was also the same month in which Homerton, Hackney Central and Hackney Wick were reopened.

9.2   FRIVOLITY AT LIVERPOOL STREET

Liverpool Street was one of a handful of stations on BR to have INTIS, the Intermediate Ticket Issuing System, as a precursor to APTIS. Whilst there were official guidelines as to the standard abbreviation to be used on Platform Tickets (a maximum of 15 characters, including class, and spaces) I had noticed that some stations on other regions were a bit inconsistent so I thought Liverpool Street ought to join in the fun.   **9-6** and **9-7**, below.

9-6

9-7

9-8

9-9

9-10

9-8, 9-9, 9-10   As far as I knew, not since Edmondson days had the separate offices at Liverpool Street been so designated, so it was time for a revival of the "Main Line" and "East Side" (also coupled with some varied descriptions.)

NOTE: The above illustrations have been reduced in size by 10%

9-11

9-12

9-11, 9-12 And finally, despite having INTIS, one Flexiprinter machine was still used in the East Side ticket office so it needed a platform ticket. I duly had the relevant part (sorry but I have completely forgotten the technical name) made for the slug, and we were in business. [See also Chapter 9.1 for my official Flexiprinter involvement.]

9.3 THE ARRIVAL OF APTIS

As by then I was Travel Centre Manager, and also Area Co-ordinator, I was one of only two persons having three APTIS keys, Operator, Supervisor and Initialisation. The AP stood for All Purpose, and it was only some time later that it came to mean Accountancy and Passenger, I'm sure coined by a less clued-up "B.R. spokesman" rather than a deliberate policy change.

9-13

9-14

9-13, 9-14 The first APTIS on the Great Eastern sector (as we had become by then) was at Ilford on 11th December 1986, but the first issues went to the BRB installation team where for once I had to stand to the side and watch! However, I got mine later in the day after they had departed and left the higher numbered machines to us locals. A point to note about APTIS is that the first issued ticket is actually 00002, because the "initialisation" card is 00000, and start of shift card 00001.

9-15

9-15 This, you have to believe, is one rarity that I had nothing whatsoever to do with! A new machine installed in the Travel Centre (while it was temporarily located where Boots is now) on 6th June 1988 showed itself as LONDON LIVERP ST when I tested the machine was in good working order by buying my customary 20 platform tickets, only to find the next morning (after the overnight electronic data transfer) it had changed to being exactly the same as the other 19, i.e. LONDON LIVRPL ST. It did not ever show this designation again, and neither did any other machine, during the time I spent there.

9-16   **9-17**

9-16 and **9-17** The APTIS programme duly proceeded, and an interesting experience occurred at Bethnal Green where my installation colleague and myself were "inside" and outside was Alan Peachey forming a queue of one for some first issues. As far as I can recall this is the only occasion on which I have "served" a fellow TTS member! The end of the programme was reached on 29 June 1989 when we had the honour of doing Emerson Park, which was the last station on BR to be converted.

NOTE: The APTIS illustrations have been reduced in size by 10%

CHAPTER 10 - DISCOVERING CZECHOSLOVAKIA

I never went to Czechoslovakia in Iron Curtain days, not making my first visit until 1991. My younger son went to the Czech Railways' 150th Anniversary in 1989, and spurred on by his reports of the number of branch lines just like Great Britain 40 years ago, very few having closed, I quickly followed in his footsteps and have now been to that part of Europe every year since. Self service ticket issue is provided at many large, and even a few small, stations in the form of Merona 7000 and 8000 machines. They have an almost identical external appearance but the print of ticket is slightly different. Their most important function, so far as I am concerned, half way down the right hand line of buttons, usually blue, is one marked "VSTUPENKA NA NASTUPISTE" (Platform Ticket). This means that sale is openly available to public purchase without having to explain your requirements at the ticket window, and end up with a flimsy paper travel ticket pretending to be a platform ticket. The insertion of a ticket roll in the machine seems to be a rather hit and miss affair, as the pre-printed logo can appear on the front or back as well as either way up! CSD stood for Československé Státne Dráhy (Czechoslovak State Railways) until the two countries split peacefully on 1 January 1993, from whence their railways became CD (Čésky Dráhy) for the Czech Republic and ZSR (Želenice Slovenskej Republiky) for Slovakia initially, which later changed to Železnicná spoločnost, as pre-printed on tickets shown at 10-5 and 12-6.

10-1

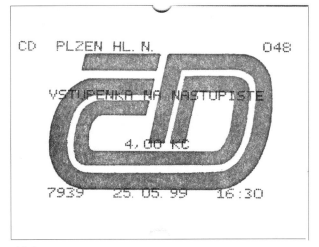

10-2

10-1 and **10-2** show examples of the more numerous type of machine, **10-1** is the former CSD logo, and **10-2** the later CD.

10-3

10-3 From Olomouc hlavni nadrazi (= main station) shows the alternative style of machine print with the miniature electric loco. The logo has come out on the back of this one due to incorrect machine loading of the paper roll. During more recent years many new passenger-operated ticket machines without a platform ticket button have been replacing the Merona, some of which have been re-located to smaller stations - see 12-5 to 12-7.

10-4   **10-5**

10-4, 10-5 Bratislava is the first ZSR logo, Zvolen the newer Zsp. where for the first time the railway title is also pre-printed on the ticket roll. Note the times in the morning when I purchased these (just changing trains!)

CHAPTER 11 - RETIREMENT YEARS - SALES AND AUCTIONS

Retirement years have been a time for consolidation in some spheres and expansion in others, especially in sales and auctions where previously unreachable gems appear from time to time.

11-1

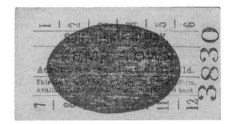

11-2

11-1 and **11-2** Some local interest first of all. Hayling Island was not issuing post 1950-ish when I tried to get them, even apparently the SR type 2 which followed the LB & SCR issue. The one illustrated is from stock which had obviously been returned to Audit earlier, another example in later years being Barcombe Mills, which also frustrated my attempts to purchase any at the station. Kemp Town is nicely dated in November 1932, just five weeks before closure, and it was good to get an issue from my nearest "branch line", and note also the similarity to the LBSCR design.

11-3

11-3 The Swindon M&SWJR is similar in a way to contemporary GWR 'BEAM' types, and perhaps a bit like the Southern "red blobs", as well as being the only issue from this joint line.

11-4

11-5

11-4, 11-5 Due to political as well as currency fluctuation in the first half of the twentieth century Germany has always come up with an interesting variety of types. Prices may be expressed in Deutschmarks, Reichsmarks, Marks, or just Pfennigs. Coloured edges, either horizontal or vertical, and often blue, are fairly numerous. The hours may be printed either way round, and the serial number can appear at either end.

11-6

11-7

11-6 Another variety of blue ends, and price in Reichsmarks.

11-7 A rather more recent machine issue, in 1958, this time with orange edges and the price only in pfennigs.

11-8

11-9

11-8, 11-9 An issue from Berlin Lehrter, one of the many stations in that city (now being re-built almost beyond recognition). Note specially, and not to be confused with the SNCF (French) end of the main station, one from Basel Bad Bahnhof, the DB station, priced at 20Rp (Swiss). [At this time the Swiss Franc and Deutschmark were almost the same value so 20 Rappen was about 20 pfennig.]

11-10

11-10 Although at school Geography and I did not get on, the former Austro-Hungarian Empire has been a source of interest to me in more recent years [see also chapter 10.] In the 1990's I have been to nearly all of the places named on these tickets. Austria, like Germany, has a history of currency fluctuation, such as 10 Kreuzer, 20 heller, etc, see on the illustrations. Pride of place in my collection is St. Polten, dry-dated on the back 29 MRZ 1893, and this ranks as the oldest platform ticket I have.

St. Polten is still very much on the map, being an important junction on the main line 60 kilometres west of Vienna.

11-11

11-12

11-13

11-14

11-11, 11-12, 11-13, 11-14 A further selection from Austria, which hopefully is self-explanatory. The Wien **11-11** is probably from the WW1 period as an unclear date appears to be 1915. **11-12** is a fairly early issue from Graz, whilst **11-13** illustrates the inflationary years of the early 'twenties. **11-14** is the same as contemporary German issues with prices expressed in Reichsmarks, and is dated 16.6.41 so from the occupation period of 1938 - 1945.

11-15, 11-16 Two from Hungary - Budapest and Szombathely, both priced 0.20 Pengo which was currency from mid-20s to 1946. Perhaps at the time of issue 0.20 Pengo was equivalent to an old English penny!

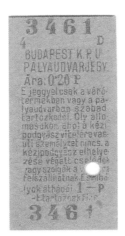

11-15

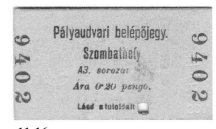

11-16

11-17

11-17 The GySEV paper ticket at 1 Forint is a mystery as it has no station back stamp. The railway still exists as it straddles the border and never became part of the Austrian or Hungarian State Railways. [After the meeting I was informed by David Veltom that the issuing station was Sopron in Hungary, the S in the railway title.]

11-18

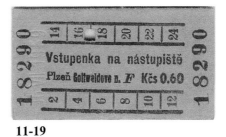

11-19

11-18, 11-19 The Czech Chomutov 1 Kc [Koruna, or Crown in English] is bi-lingual so the German on the back is also illustrated. This is most likely to date from "Empire" days as it bears some similarity to the Austrian ticket shown at 11-13. The 1956 Plzen is a post-war reduction in price to Kc 0.60, and is dated 1959, so perhaps their currency was also re-valued after 1945.

11-20, 11-21 In the Netherlands platform tickets were introduced around 1910. The examples here are a H.IJ.S.M. Haarlem 2½c, and one from Bergen op Zoom at the increased price of 5c. The system of dating seems to be day, month, and hour, which does not help to determine the year!

11-20

11-21

11-22

11-23

11-22, 11-23 The Groningen is also fairly early, but shows how types evolved, first of all by the addition of "hours" boxes. As if that wasn't enough, the press-date on the back reads "18 JUL 1N" - did they really change the type every hour? Amersfoort continued the style but shows 24-hour clock rather than a.m. and p.m. as does the Groningen. These of course pre-date my 1950 school trip (see chapter 1) by many years, at which time the price was 10c, and this subsequently rose to 20c, 25c., before, like most European countries, they disappeared altogether.

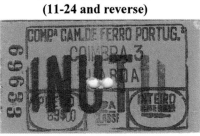

(11-24 and reverse)

(11-25 and reverse)

11-24, 11-25 Portugal seemed to already be in the re-cycling business as these examples both dated 1971 show, and the annoying thing is that I was there and didn't ask, being too busy chasing steam trains on the broad gauge and the narrow gauge, as with a BR staff holiday pass I had little need to go to ticket offices.

11-26

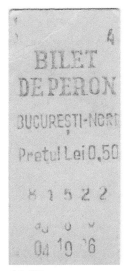

11-27

11-26, 11-27 From further afield there is Łodz in Poland, platform tickets being long gone in that country by the time I first visited there in 1994. Bucurest in Romania is still in my future plans, though, but again I do not expect to find any platform tickets still on issue.

11-28

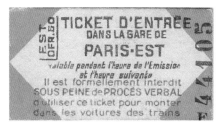

11-29

11-28, 11-29 And so back to our nearest European neighbour to round off this chapter, where those issues I have acquired over the years show that France surely surpasses Germany in the variety of styles. For a change actual railways are shown on some pre-SNCF examples, the Fecamp being from the État (State) and the Paris Est from of course the Est.

11-30 From another Paris station (not named thereon, but obviously Lyon) is yet another variation, with a bold overprint, but one needs to turn to the back to find a dry-print "P.L.M." indicating the Paris-Lyon-Mediterranée.

11-30

11-31 Many SNCF issues were of the "red edge" design, and early ones included a bold station code number for easy identification by station barrier staff.

11-31

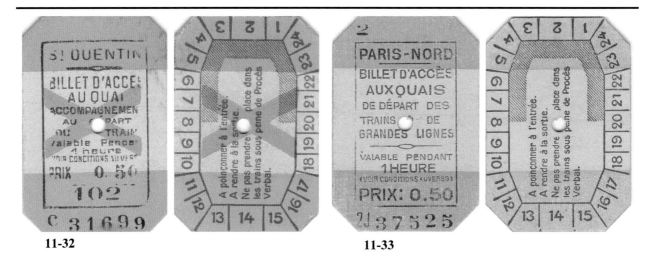

11-32   **11-33**

11-32, 11-33 It would seem that the Nord Railway had a style all of its own! St. Quentin and Paris Nord speak for themselves, and I'm not aware that any other railway produced anything quite like these. Both sides of each one are illustrated.

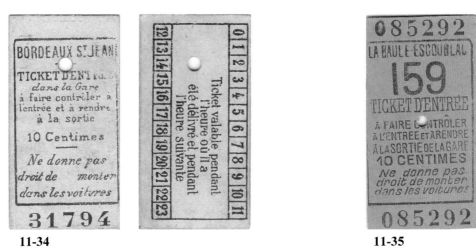

11-34   **11-35**

11-34, 11-35 Bordeaux St. Jean, on the Midi railway, like most contemporary issues, has hours boxes on the back, whilst La Baule Escoublac illustrates yet another variation on the name and number style and comes from the Paris - Orleans railway. Unfortunately there are no dates on either of these but they probably come from the inter-war period 1919 - 1939.

11-36   **11-37**

11-36, 11-37 And finally for this section, a "red blob" type from Annecy, of PLM railway origin, with a plain back and no station number, whilst Nogent-sur-Marne typifies the latter-day name and number style which evolved into name only - see 7-12 and 7-13 - until their demise in 1989.

CHAPTER 12 - INTO THE 21ST CENTURY

It seems that as the twenty-first century gets under way, platform tickets may only be found in Britain, India, and perhaps a few other places I am unaware of. This is not a 100% platform ticket talk as my interest also in remaining Edmondson cards can point you towards parts of Eastern Europe where they are alive and well.

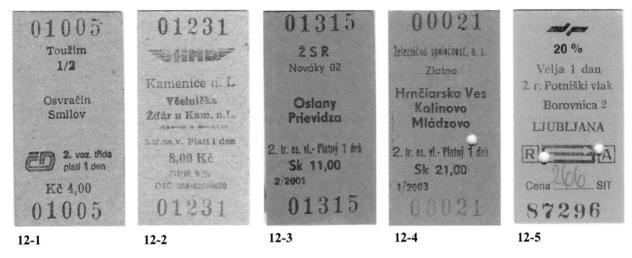

12-1   **12-2**   **12-3**   **12-4**   **12-5**

12-1 The Czech Republic (CD) still has a few of its own at very small stations which appear to be machine-less, as illustrated by Toužim, and a JHMD (a narrow gauge line based at Jindrichův Hradec) from Kamenice (**12-2**), the principal intermediate station. **12-3, 12-4** are from Slovakia (note the print date on each one) the former having the first railway title, and the second the later version as also seen at 10-5. **12-5** is from Slovenia, and Croatia also can still produce many examples (not illustrated.)

12-6

12-7

12-8

12-6, 12-7, 12-8 For platform tickets in other than the constantly changing APTIS GB, the last place in Europe is the Czech Republic and Slovakia. New issues I discovered last year [2003] were Mikulašovice stred (a most unlikely place) and Komárno, and the year before Senice na Hane - note the very low serial serial number of 16, it must have only just been put there because with the introduction of a newer type of self-service ticket machine, which unfortunately does not have a platform ticket button, old machines are being refurbished and relocated.

CONCLUSION

In the best traditions of Presidential Addresses I've done a hand-out, something for you to remember this afternoon by, a July 2004 listing of the then current situation regarding Czech and Slovak issuing stations. I hope to go there again this year to find some more that we don't know about. [But see footnote]

The end. Thank you for listening to me, and I hope I haven't bored you too much!

Les Dench

Footnote - August 2008. Sadly I have to record that 2007 and 2008 visits to the Czech Republic and Slovakia have found very few Merona machines still in situ at stations, and all of these are disconnected or display the legend "MIMO PROVOZ" which you can no doubt guess means definitely "OUT OF USE". So apart from GB, Europe is now totally without platform tickets (unless anyone knows differently.)

Picture courtesy Alan Snowdon